Peripheries

SOPHIA ALI PANDEYA

Copyright ©2015 by Sophia Ali Pandeya

ISBN-13: 978-0692506875 (Cyberhex Press)

ISBN-10: 069250687X (Peripheries)

All rights reserved. No part of this book may be used or reproduced in any manner whatsoever without written permission, except in the case of quotes for personal use and brief quotations embedded in critical articles or reviews.

Cyberhex Press

www.cyberhexpress.com

Acknowledgements

To Nayyar Jamil for nurturing the early work of myself and countless other creative minds. To Ayessha Quraishi whose art and friendship are a ceaseless source of inspiration in spite of the thousands of miles that separate us. To my brilliant muse Sascha Aurora Akhtar, for our invaluable exchanges and her fine editing on Poetry International. To the treasure that is Troy Payne for a fabulous collaboration on Lantern Journal. To Ken Bullock for his insightful critiques. To Prof. Al Filreis and everyone at ModPo-Penn for opening my eyes to the inner workings of modern poetry. To Prashant Keshavamurthy, for scholarly exchanges on Indic & Persian verse. To my mercurial genius husband Raam Pandeya for a quarter century of love, profundity and incredible food. To our beautiful sensitive son Kabir whose young sparks of poetry fill me with immeasurable joy. Many thanks to the editors of Poetry International Rotterdam, Blazevox, Lantern Journal, Elohi Gadugi, Full of Crow and Bank Heavy Press in which some of these poems have appeared previously. To my editor Matthew H. Freeman for his fine-tuned ear. To everyone at Cyberhex Press. To Sabeen Mahmud who was so cruelly snatched from us but who lives in each line of loss and remembrance.

Contents

Introduction, 7
Shipwreck, 13
Ado, 14
Among The Mother Birds, 16
Days Of The Disappeared, 19
Qibla, 20
Pall Bearer, 23
Lineage, 25
Seville Sequences, 27
Scheherazade, 33
The Green Language, 34
Girahftaar, 35
Neelum, 37
Talismans, 40
Gul Mohur, 43
Pulsing, 44
Soz, 45
Crossing the Border at Wagah, 46

Mirage, 48
Cenoté, 49
A Flight Of Paper, 50
Denim Gharara Sonata, 51
Blood Orange, 53
Citadels, 54
If You Spoke Firefly, 55
Samundari, 57
Habeas Corpus, 58
The Heart's Axis, 59
Basanti, 61
Chronicles of the Fish-Eyed Woman, 62
Lost Language, 64

Introduction

Viyogi hoga pehla kavi
— Sumitra Nandan Pant.

Periphery — ostensibly from the Greek *peripheria*, meaning "circumference, outer surface, line around a circular body" — is literally "a carrying around;" from *peripheres*, meaning "rounded, moving around, revolving," and *peripherein*, meaning "carry or move around."

The experience of moving around, of being an outsider, began early and continued throughout my life. Displacement was a multi-generational inheritance; my parents migrated from India to Pakistan in the largest exchange of populations in modern history: the violent Partition of 1947 that claimed more than a million lives. Later, in 1971, we were refugees fleeing the war when East Pakistan split off and became Bangladesh; I was nearly six at the time.

My father's work as an army doctor meant we were posted to a new city every two years. Then, in 1977, the dictator Zia ul Haq put Pakistan in the grip of martial law which sowed further chaos in our lives and led to a rupture that caused me to leave my parents' home at 21. To most western readers such a departure would be completely normal, but having grown up in a conservative Muslim society where a female is always under the "protection" of her father or husband it was nothing less than cataclysmic.

After several years of travels east and west, I migrated to the US in 1988. By the time I visited Pakistan a decade later it had become in many ways an unrecognizable place. As the saying goes, you can never go home again. Language thus becomes the most crucial possession of the exile, for it is the connection to an irretrievable past.

It is natural for the dispossessed to reflect upon what has been lost. This tendency manifests within me as an obsession with the etymology of words — the socio-historical underpinnings of the living, breathing artifact that is language. When I peel back their roots, words often trace back to Proto-Indo-European — as is the case with periphery; with *peri* being related to *paar*, the far shore, also related to *paraya* (other) the root word of pariah. *Phéré*, the plural of *phera*, to take a round, is a cognate of *phirna*, to wander.

Our common human ancestors were wanderer-gatherers and akin to them I like to yoke disparate words into new hybrid meanings. Thus the title is a double entendre: the Peri in "Peri**pheries**" referring to an archaic spelling of the Persian Pari, a mythical race of superhuman female beings, winged fairy-like creatures who are morally ambiguous which rank between angels and evil spirits.

From the Karakorum mountains of Pakistan across the Hindukush into central Asia, Afghanistan, Iran and east to India and beyond, these magical and powerful creatures are a central part of the myth and folklore of South Asia. Pari also figure abundantly in the *Dastan-é-Amir Hamza*, an enormous, sprawling, episodic Urdu romance. In folklore, the abode of the Pari is on the other side of Mount Qaf, the mountain that separates the supernatural realm from the human world. There the Pari have a kingdom from which they travel by air to the mortal world where they encounter humans and set them off on quests.

These magical, feminine, winged beings held a potent fascination, in part because they symbolized everything that I did not have while growing up: sexual agency, power, magic; but their biggest attraction was their liminal nature, moving between worlds but belonging completely to neither, a metaphor for my own existence. Thus "Peri**pheries**" dwells in the liminal, in both form and subject matter. Like the mythical, half woman half bird, it is a hybrid being. Its language, English infused with Urdu, Farsi, Sanskrit and occasionally Spanish, seeks to subvert the idea of a normative, received colonial language. In some instances, it is akin to the *sandhya bhasha* or "dusk language" of the Bengali Bauls, where meaning is nuanced, multilayered and deliberately veiled.

Sometimes the origin story of a word becomes a poem as in Blood Orange, where I mirror and marry the forgotten etymology of orange, the breakage that occurred in its journey from one language to another with the retelling of the obscure myth of the Goddess Sati — itself an epic story of fragmentation and dispersal. The act of juxtaposing one language next to another is first and foremost using language in a way that it is natural for me. Growing up bilingual has meant that it is normal to begin a sentence in one language and finish it another. Bilingualism also allows me to play with double entendre across language and dramatically enhances the sonic possibilities available to me as a poet.

Urdu is uniquely suited to this type of hybrid expression because of the ease with which its syntax can accommodate other languages. For example *"yeh* fabulous dessert *hai."* Translation: This is a fabulous dessert. The noun and adjective in this sentence are English, but the sentence as a whole is considered Urdu. Developing as an exquisitely lush heterogenous patois in North India in about the 12th century, Urdu was based on the language spoken in the region around Delhi, and it was heavily influenced by Persian and Arabic as well as Turkish.

In the lead up to and post the calamitous Partition of 1947, Urdu has fallen victim to identity politics. In India, assiduous attempts have been made to ghettoize Urdu as a solely Muslim language. In Pakistan, particularly after the advent of the obscurantist, Islamic fundamentalist military dictator Zia ul Haq, Urdu began to be systematically purged of a great deal of its indigenous vocabulary,which included words common to Farsi and and Hindi, while huge numbers of Arabic words were introduced into it. This is a process that continues even today long after the demise of Zia. For example, *Khuda Hafiz*, a term derived from Persian that for centuries had been used to say Goodbye, was suddenly changed to the ridiculously ahistorical *Allah Hafiz*, as *Khuda*, the Farsi word for God was deemed to be too ambiguous and all encompassing in its provenance, whereas *Allah* was deemed to refer only to the God of Islam. I had always been interested in understanding and decoding the roots of language, but this co-opting of God into a narrow exclusionary box was a shocking wake up call which made me realize that such an endeavor was not a luxury but a dire necessity. As language goes, so does the very foundation of our humanity.

Thus *Shipwreck*, the first poem of "Peri**pheries**" talks of: history clipped

at the wings to bury

a mongrel past

    Language is an invisible skin that clothes us from birth to death; through its fabric we are tied to history, identity, geography, politics, gender, sexuality, spirituality. To delve into these knots & undercurrents is to plumb the depths of wounds but also to encounter incomparable richness; the two are entwined and inseparable. My poetry draws from this vein of linguistic rupture and in the process tries to map how far the waters of meaning have receded, meandered or simply vanished. Poetry as forensics to diagram the labyrinths of loss by blowing Pari dust all over the partial fingerprints of history.

*   Sophia Ali Pandeya, Glen Ellen, 2015*

Shipwreck

the heart is a couplet, a twin
fracture scattered

in the shipwreck of language
she picks up an in-breath,

gulps down the clearest silence
like water needing

no translation, only
in the exhale, words
    have a country
      a meaning

they must cross &
uncross the tangled

lines, the barbs
of borders

that say *this* is Hindi, a smear
upon the other's forehead

& *this* is Urdu, a bird
we are trying to cage

in long, slender bars
of *Nastaliq*, so banished

from flight, she parrots
a false fortune

history clipped
at the wings to bury

a mongrel past

Ado

To pour out the cities
as if fluidly rearranging
pillars of salt, to sharpen
Mnemosyne's rubbled mineral

Salt as sandpaper rubbing the cryptic
into making of meaning, remember us by this
& not the disfiguring

To pour seamless, geographies, lay them out in lore,
sprout grains of Allahabad, Bhopal, Dhaka, Quetta, Sialkot,
Peshawar, Amritsar, Lahore, pour

Those whom history made an ampersand. Graveyard
of fossil salt, memory's flesh turned rose-
crystal & cold not to explore
nine-tenths below the surface, breathe
holy braille of osmosis

To pour, implore a prayer for
chronologies incarcerated in heart's erratic
place a pulse here,
in the core scripture
knot that tied you to ribcage
of aluminum whale, there you blow
maggot Jonah, blister sore, bunion on carbon
of Karachi's warm tarmac shore

To mourn, to pour
a mouthful of swallows
rebel syllable of Bangla, glissando
from your tongue's hidden corridor
heirloom of childhood's
last encore, to pour
to open this door,
with much ado, like her
who did not listen

& looked back once more.

Among The
Mother Birds

1 *Bombay Djinn*

Bombay you wrap
a sea like a sari with a mouthful

of pins, zig-zag jazz-blot damp-trot
heat-blossom of concrete underarm

drumroll of wing-flapping
warm-waltz, *pao*-drop cab-spit–

pings from Ohrmazd's sky-café
reservoire to *pissoir* of human-stream

i molt to velocities
gurgling tidal, lounge

in pigeon's brilliantine, glisten
as albino piano's eke out

a droplet of djinn and tonic-sun
you drink me

all down Bombay, carrion
in your thrum

plucked to bare bones
of solos, my scattered keys

awash at your feet rising, falling
with the egrets' music

2 Nani Konkani

Moon-Spider stayed up
all night & spun you
a coverlet of stars, *Nani*
you arose, careless, tossed
on a dawn horse and away
the stars melted like eyes fallen
in love with your glassy seas

Nani, swimming
in your swarm, cadences
are returning to my tongue like
a tide of childhood wiggling

her tiny fish-like toes

i am left & right, teeter
on those silver scales, only you
can be both, *Nani* sun-fed
enchantress who floats weight
itself, makes and breaks the glimmers,
weaves them in silks
& dusks on the changing lines
of your hand

3 Mai Kolachi

once you were *kali* comely
Kolachi, muslin wing
mother bird, diaphanous laugh
that soft woman dried

the way of wetlands
wish bone stuck
in the throat

now, you are Karachi, crisp
consonant, hard cash
claw, come to clutch
as i do. tightly

all your birds
are men, Karachi
instead of beaks, eyes
taxi

as i board the last
light they are countless
crowing

no more bird than origami yet they peck

thousands
of paper cuts, make
my skin your sea

Karachi, elegy
foaming
at the mouth

Days Of The Disappeared

the night vanished
the whispering phosphorescent wave vanished
the banana yellow dress vanished
the girl with bitten legs vanished
her father vanished
the city vanished (another took its place & went on humming)
the photo negative vanished
the used bookstore vanished
Runa Laila vanished
the names of all the roads vanished
the unannounced visitor vanished
the circular dance of digits vanished
Louise, Mary & Isabella Pinto vanished
the shape-shifting sand maidens vanished
the snake & mongoose vanished
the solitary snake charmer vanished
the mistreated bear cub vanished
the fortune-telling parrot vanished
Katrak's retail stores vanished
the benevolent monsoon vanished
the delta's singing fingers vanished
the left half of the photograph vanished
the *gul-mohur* tree vanished
Khuda, Haféz of memory vanished
the meaning of her words vanished

Qıbla

Black Stone, you promised
me in the next
world you would
have a tongue, be
a voice

For those
who touched you
the ones who walk on
unspeakable
thorns

Who could deny
the lure of mute
absolution, no
questions asked
no penances
to atone

The kiss
of stone was
soft, even as
the lips of linen on
the cusp of morning's
bone

Barely
lucid, barely
there, I stumbled
past my present
with an empty
hand

died
quietly a single
pomegranate seed
rolling in between
the folds of day and
night

Black Stone I wear
your darkness like a subtle
skin, friend, lover, sole
companion amid the
hordes that gather
chomping at
the bit

Of time's tether
spin that spits
my guts out

And yet
I cannot undo
the threads woven
in my outstretched
palms the ones
you play in catching
fishes and bubbles
and worlds that
roam

In my mind, opening
each moment like
a gift, squealing, it
is this that keeps

me going, this
that I wake to, this
that I hold
fast

Until the next
dim-time wafts
veil of indigo like
a net darkening
the waters
of sky

This is
what wraps me
entraps me sky
fish in your liminal
hour drowning
to a parallel
shore

Night, I hoard
your treasures in
my eyes, in their
deep blackness
I keep you close as
my familiar, the one
I cannot
lose

Night, you are
my touch-stone

test of spiritual gold
the one I pour
my secrets to,
the lone talisman
I hold

In between
these realms of
unstitched skin;
the naked pilgrimage
of soul

Pall Bearer

for Agha Shahid Ali, witness extraordinaire

Shahid, stop
you have blocked
all my exits. I can't
bear the weight
of your words
carry their shrouds
of white
pages anymore.

at night, the crones
come to live
in my eyes, unpack
their tightly rolled
lives and start
a smoky fire out
of the still green twigs
of disappeared sons

each name is riddle
of flame & smoke, a changing
rune I can never read
no matter how much
I cough or burn

when the grey
ash of day rubs
my eyes the old ones have
vanished, have become
stone hard dates
given at funerals

the ones that break
your teeth
if bitten

Line**age**

before you were born she skimmed
your boundary, mother
of all stripes, *linea negra*, a lean line, simple as the clean
cut that popped you, squeak & pip
of two signature lines

cradled in timbre, the line
grew shape, a skipping scribble float the *maulvi*
twisting your naughty ear to still of *bey*, made slender
letter-boat anchored by a single *nukta*
slowly you were made to form

lakeer ka faqeer, the line that would fill your life as water
does a glass, this much was clear
must memorize, repeat
line after line

no loving in this repeating
which brings us
to lineage, conundrum

at hand, look, under
the womanhood
the line you must not cross
is given, circumscribed

it hems you in from head to toe
the line, as manual, precipice, edge, abyss, endless delineation of
nots become crosses
Ash Wednesdays the forehead weathers
season after season

red and unread lines are everywhere, demarcations
of otherness, the puzzled dashes—
of word processors helpless
to corral *Alif-Laila* under their spell

when the line fell in love
it became a couplet

radif and *qafia* eloped a ghazal
that briefest of springs lingering

in between the margins
even as the line stops galloping

on the electric page
above the hospice bed

slumps two sad elbows, becomes
the four lines of the coffin
a quatrain from whose walls there is
no escape, only passage

Seville Sequences

1 llamada

What is this light?
as a feather upon my lips

Luz, light that melts
history's lozenge
upon my tongue

2 A Golpe

Ready to assume
the witness bearing pose,
I came to you

Seville, you silenced
my hand with your
cheek, humid
rukhsar turning me
back to amnion, a rumpled
spilled-skin

3 Martinetes

Climbing to *Sacromonte*
looking for the lime plaster dust
of flamenco I found
my nest-of-kin, a thousand
Anarkali's blossoming from interred frames

but, Seville, concealed
between *Al-Andalus* & *Andalucia*
your pungent conjuring zeal
that hissing mason sweat & stew
of *mudejar* & *morisco* still lives

toiling in hellish July, all
to wrap the lisp of long legged letters
into wordless prayers that rise
from porous
tongues of stone

but now I wonder, Seville, with
your curled talons of welded steel
dark-spark piercing
the heart of light; was it her, *Alba Perdita*

who became your helpless beloved?

carving you
with her very own trembling?

4 Rasgueado

Leaping ravenously
from gargoyled eaves
your feline slinking totemic,
tomcat-black

nocturnal octopi of alleyways
inked at the edge of knowledge
whiskers whisper

tickle my ear
you play me Seville, like a spell-wound toy

5 Romeras

Devil, Seville, at each corner flaunting
another street lamp Minotaur
another dangling rakish-angle
ruffle-skirted stiff whipped nun confection marzipan born
of starvation's bitter cross

in my face, my poor tourist crust
eating your centuries' concentrate
yet tasting my own
singular doom. How you taunt

haunt me with lost yet pulsing
histories, *pulpo gallego*, ink of eon
swarm-arm of Tantalus tentacled arc
tantu of freshly sundered air, where
I too am some of sum, *ung* hung in tapestry of your trapeze,
open-ended ease, *balanceo*

                  y vaivén

            you swing, Seville
                  suddenly reveal, with a staccato tap

your horizon's fan, unfurled
where tireless tribes of *tablaos* clap
callused hands & feet like hoofbeats slap-galloping
horses of their thighs

in your wheel,
Seville, time is nothing

but a moon-faced clock

even your crowds are castanets cantering
down the steps

everywhere, is the dance, the dance
is everywhere

6 Braceo

Solemn synonyms, your balconies field
cards held close to crop
afternoon's hard shot glass

but at the onset of that *orujo* known as evening
the jute eyelids disappear, spear
a new slivered swordfish swum
in blue-mirrored window & underneath,
the triumphal palm become emblem
of a withering crucified Issa
until next year's *Santa Semana*

& beneath all,
the convoluted under bellies of eight hundred egg white & lapis
years

Jubilant Seville
whose Thursdays are thirst days
holy relics consecrated with wine and thine
& clapping apparitions masquerading as furniture restorers
& certain old men & certain young men
& iconic barbers. How is it possible?
the dare of your elderly Alcazar
who does not collapse
under jasmine's young
& head strong weight?

7 Peteneras

Seville, behind your heavy, metal-nippled doors
dour balding patriarchs reluctantly bestow
spidery lace on brides and widows
from their high perches *mantillas,*
mantones & regalos flash plumage of gold and cream barely
cupped in the iris of a dream

and in certain obscure recessed
arm-lengthenings of evening shadow *taparias*
are grown men who have labored

in decades long solitude
over the meaning of a fig, the precise
nose of a *rioja*

8 Fandango

faraway yet near there are
newborn rooms
where *papier maché* bulls
snort, sport newspaper, suspend reality, proclaim
y bella y bestia
as if every pedestrian was
a toreador

9 Melisma

on certain uncertain bone
chipped plastic tables lies a lone
blood red paper shell
crushed, consummated empty as a siesta
Senor Tabac mourns his warning: *La muerte lenta
y dolorosa*... O, to die

in the arms of such a language

10 Siguiriyas

Seville, you will
be you, but I drank
& now, Mnemosyne,

I *Salud*, drown
in your drams, of delicate
& curlicued gloom, faded
yet blinding bloom, rose in the mile-stone

teeth of Guadalquivir

Scheherazade

At twenty, tiring
of made up stories
that climbed the endless loop
of sleep and waking

I dreamed of her, archaic yet urbane,
a name that could be construed either way:
Sheher-azade: She-who-set-the-city-free
like so many birds uncaged, daughters of daughters
streaming in spinnerets of every ilk

Or was she Sheher-zade: a city-bound
heart's hammered words
trying to pry open the pad-
locked arms of sky?

Well, I tell you now
I have swallowed both meanings,
that minaret sword, that fruited sun,
an inverted dome, a weeping onion
shedding all my skins,
one by silent one

I have let down my ladders, run
the tightrope, clung to myself
at each rung and now

I know precisely the quality of absence
The street shall wash its hands of me
as if morning was an hour made of sand
and time will put memory to sleep
like a rabid dog

The Green Language

We know the green language, you and I
The one that speaks in sentences of light

Summer's currency a freckled gold
Peaking on the eggshell cheeks of sky

We know the green language, you and I
Wind that whips the leaves off autumn's lips

In hungry licks and slow full-circled sips
Swirling gently at our feet like dervish sighs

We know the green language, you and I
We are pilgrims of the unmarked shrines

Made and unmade on the shores of skin
We are mendicants of madness, the loud

Silence of atoms, moving yet still
Beating in the hearts of bearded banyans

Hollow as armpits, holding us aloft
While the city speeds by, numinous unaware

We know the green language, you and I
The one that turns ochre, crimson, vermilion

And burnt sienna, on the pages of our eyes
The one that knows us, knows the ache

As we leave these rooms of leaf and roots
Slowly bleeding off the margins of time.

Girahftaar

She dwells
in borders, imbroglio of tangling
tresses drunk, snaking to become
a warming lake's waning
hairline

how shallow to pulse
as abacus, count a birth
day marked as *saal-
girah*, yet another
year-knot tied
in life's slowly
shortening
string

strings are cut
at birth, the first knot
tied and stilled, on tiny balloon
of belly receding
into dark navel-seed
from which, unruly as weed
to be tamed and named
everything turns

to stone one day, its all in
the in between, the lean
to lightning, much maligned
tongue *patung* to cut cataract, gaze
as crucible, catalyst
to chrysalid, seethe

she breathes up from
the deep, her wreath
of serpents now awaking
coiled multitudes
of sleep to the ends
that must
arrest

Neelum

Was there a river? Her lake
is landlocked butterfly
monadnock of mountain turquoise swimming
in skull, *kokh* of veined throb
continually stillborn

Cradled in ore
in plump and flesh history is
one such milling and she, granular
descent, walk but careful
to place a crystalline surrender in
the crawl of jasmine's pliable tendril
grow a slow pearl, fracture set
against grit of ember
inching to flame

But if not if knot if not if knot if not
if love's a seismic inflorescence
then what, must shatter. No
just dust

Oh, how she smites!
her smiles seam-stressing borders of tiny, even
as an ear worm clambers in, rises
from the torque of her, spinneret
of Arachne, a talisman she knows
only as second hand memory, Partition's opaque sea
a looking glass resting in uneasy pieces

Her five fingers are
animal paw, they make rivers, shrines
to freshly blown songs of bread, celebrate
that which is broken
midstream, her lips trace
taste of geometry lost amid the torched
hexagrams of Damascus

There are eyes everywhere
they braid the salt of her body into ribbons
woman as aubergine as evening's
habitually violet tongue
she is a night shade, *Neelum* who wishes
that mother indigo had weaned her, warned her, watch

Out for the changing lines, they are pulled
set apart he & she are they & it is
finally a migrant problem. The job is to stand

wrap the sands of time into aluminum foil
warp & weft & warp & weft & slap
the miracle of fishes is floundering now
nail beds as tumulus of rare minerals
Catacombs of Silica. Do not discard. Do not swallow.
Swallow. Who goes up in flames from
behind the headlights? Let me write
the answer for you, that yes
is actually why

Tunis is blue-
print of your palm
plant of rogue fortune teller, how else
could lifelines made of dirt
and coffee be fertile grounds of your death
which blooms everyday in that lush gauntlet, checkout line

32 thousand spent shells and each day the sky
sheds only a lone blood-stop that fails
to arrest and each day the night
presses a solitary coin, hush money

on your tongue. *Hikmet* weeps oceans
of verse but all his pigeon grey tears
are bayoneted leaflets you try to fashion
into lifeboats but still they flock about you, capsized
as only small print could be

Every drowning is a dove
of yesterday's newspaper she folds
the dead up like origami and sleeps
in their sheet. There, you have your lapel
a flower pinned neatly down. She is a specimen. You are a Phd
crossing the throat of the Bosphorus
ever so calmly

While she is Googoosh, ghost that rewinds
like all nightingales *mirabilis*
in little plastic attics, inhales
relic as corsage of static's kiss
and evening's industrial duckling melts
wafts of night waxing in the wings
flight of memory's plane is Icarus
ululating yellow taxi, land-
locked lip to plumb
mouths of gaps
endlessly

Talismans

1 *Fleur de Sel*

the first memory was a white
blindness a braille of
salt that water leaves
behind like a wayward lover making
a trail of tell-tale deserts
in his path a slow burning writes
scrolls on your cheeks a garland
of tiny skulls holds
the dark ocean you crossed
to become this flower

2 *Dispersal*

the windshield is
a cinema raindrops
patrons throngs arriving
leaving arriving I cannot
look not now not
ever says a muffled
voice in the back before
the shatter all rain
begins as rime hexagon
prism seed spell snow
grows in your sky
womb until crystal
succumbs

3 Zephyr

it grows against all odds, a weed
wherever water can gain a foothold, a blade
of grass or a lone dandelion moaning
in the crack of asphalt dawn a flower
in the night with no windows a sky that shudders
and shutters all its stars in grey
cloud burqas it is – and you are – this
and also that – an adamant
agate – buraq – the zephyr
breathing on your little
finger while the chain
still dangles, smiling from
the unlatched door

4 Henna-fish

confluent as the lines of your hands once
were, clenched tightly as you struggled
against the itch the urge to open
your palms to the skies and catch
the next rain of thought henna-fish
will be lost and never found
again on these tracks there must
be borders or else chaos ruins
the filigree she warned squeezing
drops of clove tea over the drying
islands I told her I was writing
a labyrinth without maps she said
everything is a thread that unravels

5 Saturn's Rings

my skin and yours are borders
where the stories lie sleeping
curled up like cats in the solemn
afternoons of our mating what is
left of these shrines are just
grimy circumambulations
Saturn's rings on my bathtub
of nine lives time and
time again I slit
my mind in this
brine until we are
one my skin as
wrinkled as your
ancient hide
and seek

6 Archeoseti

I am Tethys' whorling
ellipsis, the kiss
of marine phosphorescence
a swarm of swaying
baleen whose prayers are
teeth of endless rosaries
whispering 'tamtu , tamtu'
into the deep indigo that
neither day nor night
can catch

Gul Mohur

Somewhere, in her city by the sea
rains have fallen, all at once
like a tongue long held
spilled a torrent of love and hate and curses
loud enough to wake the dead
shivering in their waterlogged graves
somewhere in her city by the sea
rains have fallen
on keepers of arboreal wisdom,
that delicate filigree of long necked acacias
listening to the sky
has tattered
has scattered orange anagrams on
the rages of street-rivers
the water noising like a thousand tongues
somewhere in her city by the sea
rains have fallen
cold as a secret in a lost child's clenched
palm, the rain has taken, as the sun did before
her, and the hunger before then and looming
yes, death, but also life, the air cool as a
morning stone, frogs jumping in exclamation
points, the sweet scent of earth's yielding
somewhere in her city by the sea
rains have fallen, left
a damp exhale she wears
like a moth eaten shawl
on her shoulders

Pu**lsing**

dear ear
dear *humdum* humdrum
dear absorption, dear amplitude of libidinous
dear dearly departed, dear hash-tagged post-age, dear hurl of tiny url
dear cooped up, dear coin cup, dear manna hatter, dear syringe in sky, dear patient ether dear death by thousand cut-edit-paste
dear denizen, dear muddling middle
dear ambiguity
dear un-redressed unrest
dear *lub* of labyrinth, dear minotaur of Mnemosyne
dear daddy, dear oscillating ossuary, dear bone of contention
dear horror dear drone, dear hour, dear *rouh*
dear abbreviated amp-mutated, dear history
dear cut-off midstream, dear of beat off beat
dear torrent, dear DADA, dear lyric neurotransmitter
dear hastily assembled, dear pastiche
dear archaic, dear air, dear Baudelaire, dear Drunken Boat, dear Rimbaud rainbow,
dear OULIPO
dear accretion, acceleration, debacle, dear chewed up metonym
dear line, dear seer, dear linear, dear antonym of dead ant, dear luggage
dear dangling, dear language, dear lengthening, dear feral un-furled, unending
dear eye of cursor, pulsing
                    pulsing

Soz

She dwells in iris, of urdu
nargisi necropolis, mirror

of history's orb webs
time she telescopes by *tilism*

plumes a mane of dust to dirge
alaap of *alif's* spindling syllable

glossolalia leaps a gap, gulps
an ossuary fire, *soz* of wish-bone

Crossing the
Border at Wagah

Yamī appears
a full twenty-one days before
we cross over to *that* side, mother

of leather trunks, a black, pot-bellied
buffalo spreading her bovine
domain in Bia's bedroom, her guts
neatly sausaged *malmal*
dupattas destined to be disemboweled
billow in whim of changing ratios
saris to *shalwar kameez*
segments, sediments, sentiments
time's running stitch she wears
as it wears her
down & down
the parallel sun-
sets of hands rolling
sleeves like wheels

at Lahore station emerging
from that laughable misnomer known
as *Tézgaam*, the swift footed
coolies flock us, scarlet turbans wedded
like new brides to weight, balance the proverbial
water buffalo on their heads, sprint
up the platform steps

to tame a taxi,
tether her at torso
mother atop
& mother below
mutter a prayer
snake through
traffic's chokehold on Mughal afterglow
to rendezvous with our twin baggage
seismic siamese birth canal
the Grand Trunk Road
now lone umbilicus
between us, yoked
to spike & separate
gates in Pakistan

& India, where suddenly
time is a dropped
stitch, that other half, now
past, twitches briefly on
her watch before turning
back to palm
a phantom limb

Mirage

Voltaic tongue-sten bulb in my mouth
Your mouth where the roots burrow deep

As daikon swords in the sunless places
Sibilance of ploughs unfurling my petulance

As I split earth furrows I am drowning in
Your sleep pendulous in thick of noon

At the knee of upheaval's peak and snow
Appeared like a mirage like a pause before

Death perhaps the same moment as
Repentance would alight like a

Night moth upon your eyes except now
My eyes are turbulence are thrust are

Speaking at last my lost chapters
To the tumult of your fallen skies

Cenoté

As a child,
you collected ways
not dolls
rolls of owl
a waking's call

now peals
back to dark, whittles
bark, stokes heart-
wood to sputter, burns
midnight's charcoal

fingers until utter
sparks, fires off
hissing folios, damp
herstory curling

logic's manual, jumps
script – offers Minerva
a blue ear, begging bowl, *cenoté*
to altar of sonar

you sink, she wells, up-
rising, close –
eyes, listen

A Flight Of Paper

On the chaotic street
elderly electrical poles are holding
up a tangle of teeming wires like
abandoned games of Cat's
Cradle on the chaotic

street the wind is an unpaid
typist i am an orphan unpacking
the furious shorthand of her riprap

cracking open
the knuckles of shuttered
light, missives lying all over as
if every lost cat was
a flight of paper

on the chaotic street
clouds of kite messengers are doomed
to be cut like a child's
tiny scissored laughter

on the chaotic street Haruki
is folding me in his
arms as if i was
origami

on the chaotic street i am
a nuclear rose a thousand
petaled poem going up
in flames

Denim Gharara
Sonata

I am dreaming of a denim *gharara* with accordion
pleats that a Catalan gypsy named Pascal
is playing
his wizened Olympian hands wear
a ring for each continent while Amalia
sings a *fado* in a far corner under
an interrogation-hot spotlight but somehow
her voice is blooming in my ear like a loud red
flower i am dreaming

of a denim *gharara* studded
with steel grommets you can open
and close the accordion bars like musical
notes with leather gladiator thongs Russell
Crowe is not in this dream nor is Charlton
Heston, no, the fringes are eyelashes
of a teenage Baloch boy who makes
the world's most beautiful shoes out of
old tires and sacrificed
rawhide his copper face is missing
two teeth and smiles at me, disembodied as
he disappears like a penny
in a wishing well, now *farshi*

the denim *gharara* has transformed
into a flamenco dancer's train, the accordion
is a harmonium is a whirlpool whose iris
pleats give a mighty monocled wink before
swallowing Pascal whole in their
hole where i catch a last glimpse of the crooning
Runa Laila the denim *gharara* is a blotting
paper fan

a wingspan drunk on a rainbow
of chemical soup my teeth
are made of castanet-nails and slowly
sinking in brass
brigadiers have stolen all
the grommets of my denim
gharara before drowning i remember
the Baloch boy's name it's the same
as mine.

Blood **Orange**

As her words broke, I licked
laal on my lips, *khooni* mix
of elixir with pip, lexeme's

tasalsul cracked
from eggshells, yoke's echo
a slippery new born *shums*
lightling *lafz*, solitude's syllable

she, *gul*, arabesque
multitude of arms, legs, fingers, torsos
& worlds of tongues become honeycomb
kalam melisma tumbling cumulus tumult
catapulted cartwheeling unruly consonants grinning
from ear to shaft of *shabd*, come in sinew
of ambidextrous rooting
sutradhars in deep throated knit & purl

what ribbons finally, finely as
her water's mirror calm, swum
to *sagar* of slow kneaded wholeness, the words
like hallowed bread, *alfaaz*
rising above themselves
her *hurf* self-seeding seminal feminine
from *Narangi* to *Naranjo* & then
like an umbilical stem
the nascent n snaps

& orange rolls, round
dimpled and english
out of our mouths

Citadels

To sack a city, first storm
its citadels
pick up the words

examine their inlets
look deep into their spring
loaded green eyes

If You Spoke
Firefly

If you spoke firefly
flicked a remorse code
on and off like a
leaf-tongue leaning
to the changing breeze

The fluencies implicit
in paced pentets
double pulses
separated by three

Rounds of darkness, the
flashes bleating
like skipped
heartbeats as you calyxed
close to the node, the
confluence held

If you spoke firefly
came down
like *pyractomena angulata*
in a flickering orange rain
on the skin of darkness

A call and response threading
the domain of otherwise
invisible lovers whose
desire reaped visceral

Victuals, coiled
nuptial gifts glowing
on their bellies, harbingers
of many joysorrows bundled
like hurried bedding
as they fled
into themselves

If you spoke firefly
would I be
a lapsed
synapse lost
like a shoelace in
the singing gardens of night?

Samundari

A bird called ocean, knocks
upon your land
clocked window where days
march like armies, in
a long single file
following sugar's real
or imagined crystal

She presses
in *peripheries*, wings
like rain across your glass
desert, pours in endless
waves, breaking

open veins within
flow unfettered from
taps choking on air's
narrow wind pipes

Samundari runs away
with your footprints, walks
in sea-foam riddles
that disappear
as you decipher, curl

her toes into seashells, listen
for the chrysalid hum
in bone, bird

as oriflamme, salt spray
of feathers swirling
your neck where once
like Ma'at, the weight
of angels perched

Habeas **Corpus**

Produce the body, her delicate coinage laid
out as dowry would be, for all to examine

Richness of loss, touch her mongrel flair
curve of missing column, absent *shair*

The Heart's Axis

This globe's a top
I have spun
on heart's axis

oscillating

a butterfly curve
swum on my finger
as last blind whorl
of dolphins in
the river's plume

came singing

your open mouth
the delta spilled
a peacock's fan
ethereal in the

early dawning

that found us
crooked as
elbows of cedars
knotted in our

span of kneeling

trunk and tributary
slung, swash
and backwash

we clung

sublingual in our
littoral drift
our kites were tongues
that kissed, but
also cut like
mouths of glass

whistling

Basanti

Eye-lashed to a line of Khusrau
Lode of *gul-e-ashrafi* ore

Her begging bowl, sugar skull split
(S)tongue narcotic, nacreous core

Chrono-some's, double barreled helix
Cross-hairs of djinn-puns, *paan az*

*Zubaan-**é**-zeest,* scatter-spun *dhun*
Zurd-sun's twin-petal wing-burn

Blooms *basanti*, bursts constellations
Streams in zest-tempestuous seams

Phool rahi sarson sakal bun
February, memory's *pari*

Chronicles of the
Fish-Eyed Woman

Each nightfall she braids
three rivers into rungs
of silence, anchors
their throttled shores to a stray
tendril of sky
and climbs

On the other side of water's
mirror the moon's fallen
copper is a keening wish
fulfilled, the sacrament
ash of vanished worlds
made poems

On the fourteenth night
you find her living lip
to ripple, spinning rivers
of dark-tressed words flagrant
as any moon's lover
but grim

Velocities of day
break every bone of night's
shining china, her poems
slump in lisps of worthless
paper, crumpled coinage
of the realm

Of silver and yet many
many moons later, after the delta
has died in fistfuls and left her
storied reams

The threads of rivers scribbled
as grey ghosts on the banks
of her shoulders she still
sky-dives into that infinite well
deep where she breathes, weaves the vivid
ink of dreams

Lost **Language**

I, the swallower of fishes
came from the south, the
unencumbered country of
your tongue, of stone-feathered
sentences spreading out in the
slow making heat the unending
paragraphs of the monsoon

You, shedding loads but the
electricity never left your fingers
what came to mind was archaic,
gulqand made with rose petals
and honey spread out to dry in the
moonlight which itself became a
tongue speaking a lost language...

www.ingramcontent.com/pod-product-compliance
Lightning Source LLC
Chambersburg PA
CBHW061343040426
42444CB00011B/3066